A souvenir guide

Bath Skyline
Somerset

Robin Dixon, Amy Feldman, David Goode,
Martin Papworth

National Trust

Mary Berry's Bath

The first thing you notice on the Bath Skyline walk is the view.

The entirety of the Georgian city laid out before you: elegant cream, Bath-stone buildings trickling out from the huge medieval Abbey with its unmistakable, magnificent stained-glass windows.

The second is how peaceful it is there. These calm, wildflower-filled fields couldn't feel more removed from the rest of the bustling UNESCO World Heritage Site in your eye line.

I was born in Bath in 1935, was at school and college there and I still think of it as home. My father used to say Bath was like Rome – surrounded by seven hills.

I'm not the only person to have forged fond memories here. Ever since Jane Austen and her contemporaries came to these hills some two hundred years ago, the countryside surrounding Bath has provided a respite from city living. On any given day you might find a family kite-flying, a couple walking their dog through Smallcombe Wood, a runner absorbed in their own world.

The six-mile trail devised by the National Trust can be savoured in sections: a lunchtime picnic next to Sham Castle; testing the seesaws in the Woodland Play Area; or it can be embraced in one trek, plenty of ascents and descents. The latter option is a challenge, but undeniably a rewarding one. You'll stumble across wooded valleys, spy a Roman hill fort and might spot pyramidal or bee orchids, or marbled white butterflies flitting among the carpet of wild flowers. Bath University has even found that completing the walk burns off more than 700 calories – the same as a 90-minute football game or an hour of swimming. So be sure to treat yourself to a slice of Victoria sponge once you've finished, at one of the many tea-rooms back in the city centre!

As you make your way to the Skyline and the clamour of the city subsides, you can understand why the Georgians liked to come out here to 'take the air'. That's not to say that I don't savour the delights of all that urban Bath has to offer. But there's something special about being able to walk just a mile or two and feel like you're in this totally different world.

To me Bath centre is Milsom Street and the many regal Georgian buildings surrounding it. Remember to look up at the architecture, especially when moving farther afield to the Circus to admire the acorns capping the tops of the balustrades. Look up to the sky and embrace the rooftops. I am sure you will be touched by Bath, just as I have been all my life – now get your walking boots on!

Best wishes

Mary Berry

Welcome to Bath

Along with its Roman baths, historic Abbey and honey-coloured stone buildings, Bath's surrounding countryside is one of its most distinctive – and beloved – features.

The surrounding hills can be seen from almost anywhere in the UNESCO World Heritage Site. In fact, they were part of the very reason the city earned its international designation, joining Venice, Italy as the only other site where city and setting share the world heritage inscription. These expanses of green are just waiting to be explored; even though they might look distant, the countryside surrounding Bath begins less than one mile from the Abbey, and is easily accessible by bus or foot.

The power of fresh air
Although you can't really miss seeing this panoramic lush setting, in such a history-rich city it's easy to get distracted by the many other delights on offer and for the hills to fade into the background. But not only does the countryside

Above **Looking out over Bath from the Skyline in autumn**

Opposite above **A watercolour of Bath cathedral by Nick Hirst**

Opposite below **A group of children enjoying the Woodland Play Area, part of the Bath Skyline (see page 53)**

have a rich history of its own – much of which is revealed in this guidebook – we now know it has the power to make us healthier, less stressed and even improve our self-esteem and sense of self-worth. Put most simply, it makes us happier and, as Octavia Hill suggested over one hundred years ago, we need it. What better reason is there for the Trust to continue looking after these places and make them accessible for everyone, for ever – and for you to strap on your boots and explore them?

When you do so on the Bath Skyline, you'll discover flower-strewn summer meadows, fields perfect for kite-flying, woodland walks and picnic spots with a view. There's a purpose-built Woodland Play Area to run around in and hilltops with a history that pre-dates even the Romans. This guidebook provides an insight into each area, from stories about its past to the wildlife you might spot there today. You'll discover the

site of a deadly duel and where to spot bats. You'll find out where there were once busy horse-racing days before the course at Lansdown was built, where Bath stone was once quarried, and which birds to look out for during your walk.

This is all accompanied by step-by-step guides to two walks and a Family Discovery Trail, all of which are waymarked. Walk to the View guides you from the city centre to the countryside. The six-mile Bath Skyline walk offers varied terrain with far-reaching views across the city. Whether you're heading out today, or just starting to plan your trip, we hope this guidebook encourages you to join us in the hills.

'The need of quiet, the need of air, and I believe the sight of sky and of things growing, seem human needs, common to all men'

Octavia Hill, co-founder of the National Trust, 'More Air for London', 1888

The National Trust in Bath: a timeline
The National Trust owns 202 hectares (500 acres) of countryside in Bath, or 10% of the UNESCO World Heritage Site, with land having been acquired from 1930 onwards.

1930: Little Solsbury Hill donated by the Hicks family

1931: Bath Assembly Rooms donated by Mr E. E. Cook

1959: Rainbow Wood Farm, Claverton Down and, in 1960, Bushey Norwood donated by Mrs Mallet

1984: Bath Skyline (Smallcombe Vale, Bathwick Fields, Bathwick Wood) acquired through public appeal and a £100,000 donation from Bath Council

1993: Prior Park Landscape Garden, donated by the Christian Brothers and Prior Park College

2016: Hancock's Land bought with thanks to two generous bequests in aid of improving access to the countryside

A Brief History of Bath

Above The west front of Bath Abbey features unique ladders of angels. It's said the first Bishop of Bath had dreams of angels ascending and descending into heaven, which inspired him to build a new Abbey church

In the minds of our ancestors, Bath was a rare, wonderful and magical place where hot water came out of the ground without human influence.

No wonder the god of the spring required worship, and prehistoric objects, including Iron Age coins, were cast into the hot water long before the Romans were here.

The earliest inhabitants

Evidence has been found of prehistoric human activity in Bath from c.2800BC onwards, including Bronze Age round barrows and Iron Age farmsteads. These inhabitants may have been attracted by the light limestone soils surrounding the city, which were ideal for early cultivation using the ploughs of the time.

The Romans arrive

Following their invasion of Britain in AD49, the Romans developed Bath's hot springs into Aquae Sulis, a spa and religious centre renowned throughout the Roman Empire. They created a monumental shrine complex to worship the Celtic goddess Sulis. The area became a site of pilgrimage from far and wide. By the end of their tenure they had established the first defensive walls around the city, a boundary that would come to define the settlement's limits for the next 1,300 years.

The Saxon and Norman city

The Romans left Britain in AD410. Under Saxon rule, Bath – now encircled by the Roman wall – became an important monastic town with a prestigious Abbey and local mint. The first King of all England, King Edgar, was even crowned in Bath Abbey in 973.

Following the Norman Conquest of 1066, John de Villula of Tours, the first bishop of Bath (see page 10), embarked on a major rebuilding programme that transformed the city into a well-known centre for healing and the Christian faith.

Early industries

During the 12th and 13th centuries, Bath gradually lost status as an important cathedral city. Instead it flourished as a small, moderately prosperous centre for the wool trade and cloth industry until decline set in from the 16th century.

The decline of religion

Following the dissolution of the monasteries in the 1530s, Bath's ecclesiastical authorities lost their powers to the city corporation and most monastic land and property was sold off by the crown. The citizens of Bath acquired increased control over their affairs. The city began to regain its status as an important health resort and in the late 17th century, became increasingly attractive to the social elite.

Above Statues looking over the 'Great Bath', the centrepiece of the Roman Baths where Romans bathed in hot spa water

The Georgian party town

By the early 18th century, Bath had established itself as Britain's leading recreational resort for the rich and fashionable and there was a growing demand for seasonal accommodation and entertainment for wealthy visitors.

'Fine balls and fine concerts, fine buildings, and springs
Fine walks, and fine views, and a thousand fine things,
Not to mention the sweet situation and air,
What place, my dear mother, with Bath can compare?'

Extract from a poem in *The New Bath Guide,* Anstey, 1766

From 1720–93, the city's fabric was transformed, its alley-like medieval streets replaced with elegant Palladian squares, terraces, crescents, pleasure gardens and assembly rooms. Entrepreneurs such as John Wood the Elder and Ralph Allen (see page 10), as well as the city corporation and emerging financial institutions, all further stimulated growth. By 1801, the city had become the eighth largest in England; its population had risen from just over 2,000 at the beginning of the 18th century to 35,000, swollen by wealthy visitors, and the labouring classes and lower orders of society who served them. In the 19th century, Bath became a place of permanent residence for the wealthy upper and middle classes.

Industrial growth

At the same time, the city developed a strong industrial and commercial sector. New industries such as engineering and printing were established and Bath developed an international reputation for cranes. The opening of the Kennet and Avon Canal in 1810 and the Great Western Railway in 1840 expanded the city's transport and communication links. A revival of Bath's spa was well under-way by the 1880s.

20th-century Bath

In the 20th century, further industries were developed in Bath and the service sector expanded to meet the needs of mass tourism. Finally, in 1987 Bath's cultural and architectural heritage was recognised through the city's inclusion in the list of UNESCO World Heritage Sites.

Opposite 'Comforts of Bath, Plate 2' by Thomas Rowlandson, 1798. Rowlandson was a well-known English artist and caricaturist, and this print is taken from the second edition of Rowlandson's 'Satires'

Left An aerial view of Bath, including the Royal Crescent and Circus

The creators of Bath

A number of key figures helped shape Bath into the city you might recognise today.

John de Villula (d.1122)

Also known as John of Tours (he was born in the French city), John de Villula was a medical doctor and ordained priest. He became Bath's first bishop in 1091 and by 1098 John had received ownership of the entire city, then much ruined, from William II and begun a major redevelopment scheme. This included the construction of a vast new Abbey church and cathedral, monastic buildings, a Norman deer park and refurbished hot baths. John's plans, mostly completed between 1136 and 1166, greatly revitalised Bath as a health spa and Christian centre.

Ralph Allen (1693–1764)

Cornish-born Ralph Allen was a highly successful businessman. He moved to Bath at a young age and remained there for the rest of his life. Having joined the city's postal service, he made his fortune from developing the national network of postal routes.

Allen is a big part of the reason Bath is now a World Heritage Site: his local quarries (see page 29) provided the honey-coloured stone for many of Bath's famous 18th-century streets and squares. He also donated money to local charities, including the city's general hospital, and enthusiastically supported the arts. In the 1730s, he commissioned Prior Park, a magnificent Palladian mansion overlooking the city, with landscaped gardens and a 1,200-hectare (3,000-acre) estate (see pages 42–5).

John Wood the Elder (1704–54)

The architect and town planner was born in Bath, the son of a local builder. Aged 21, he left the city to pursue a career in architecture, first in London, then Yorkshire. Having developed a passion for Palladian architecture and Ancient British history, he returned to Bath in 1727 with an extraordinary plan to restore it as a great classical city, inspired by its ancient Roman predecessor. His major designs include Queen Square (1728–35), Ralph Allen's Prior Park (c.1733–51) – one of the finest examples of English Palladianism, the North and South Parades (1739–48) and the Circus (1739–48), Britain's first circular street.

John Wood the Younger (1728–82)

In his early years, John the Younger worked closely with his father, John the Elder. His independent career began with the development of the Circus, which was unfinished on his father's death. Next he designed and built Gay Street to link the Circus with Queen Square. Later, using a less ornate Neo-classical style of architecture than his father, Wood created a number of new buildings and terraces in Bath, including the New Assembly Rooms and much of Bath's Upper Town. Arguably his greatest achievement was the Royal Crescent which, in contrast to traditional squares, was an outward-facing composition that for the first time allowed every resident to overlook a rural prospect, as if in a country house. Such crescent-shaped terraces were to become very influential in town design.

Top left Ralph Allen's Prior Park

Top right Ralph Allen, depicted by William Hoare in 1742

Middle left John Wood the Elder's Circus, which was completed by his son

Middle right The Royal Crescent, designed by John Wood the Younger

Bottom Richard 'Beau' Nash, after William Hoare, oil on canvas, c.1761

Richard 'Beau' Nash (1674–1761)

The self-styled 'King of Bath' is often credited with the city's explosion in popularity in the 18th century.

Nash arrived at Bath in 1705, having dropped out of university and abandoned two careers. He had a passion for gambling and a talent for organising successful social events. Soon after he moved here, he became the city's Master of Ceremonies, a position he held until his death. At the time, Masters of Ceremonies were responsible for ensuring society mingled amicably and for the next 50 years Nash engagingly but forcefully encouraged civil behaviour among all visitors to the city with the help of his famous code of polite conduct, 'Rules to be observ'd at Bath'. It was said that 'even the royal family themselves had not influence enough to make him deviate from any of these rules' (Oliver Goldsmith, 1762).

Later, scandals and advancing age undermined Nash's role as social leader and arbiter. He died in debt.

'10. That all whisperers of lies, and scandal, be taken for their authors'

One of Beau Nash's behaviour rules for Bath

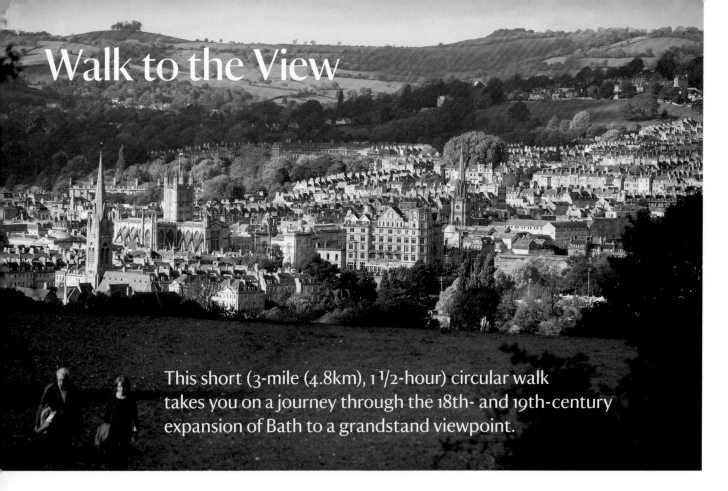

Walk to the View

This short (3-mile (4.8km), 1 1/2-hour) circular walk takes you on a journey through the 18th- and 19th-century expansion of Bath to a grandstand viewpoint.

The Georgians often visited Bath's hills to escape the hubbub of the city and 'take the air'. Starting at the Visitor Information Centre, you'll follow in their footsteps as you pass 18th-century landmarks such as Great Pulteney Street and Sydney Gardens, and will discover the tranquil setting of Bath's canal, before finishing on Bathwick Fields, with a panorama of the city and countryside before you.

1727: the development of Bath

By the second quarter of the 18th century, much was happening of great importance for Bath's future transformation from cramped medieval town to spacious Palladian city. The architect

John Wood the Elder was planning to build Queen Square, the first major accomplishment in Bath's 18th-century redevelopment. At the same time, Ralph Allen was purchasing the Combe Down quarries, soon to become the largest source of building stone for Bath's great reconstruction (see pages 8–11).

Ralph Allen's town house (Nos 1 and 2 North Parade Passage)

Allen was making a name for himself as a precocious and capable postmaster of Bath and from 1718 he was a sub-tenant here. The building became the headquarters for his postmaster works and, after acquiring the lease in 1727,

Above Visitors walking on Bathwick Fields, part of the Skyline route, with the view to Bath beyond he added a Palladian façade to the rear. On its north side, he built a detached wing with a similar but more elaborate design; it was from here that he probably ran his postal business for a while. These buildings are visible through the gate adjacent to the Friends' Meeting House in York Street.

Parade Gardens

Lying just outside the city wall, this was once an orchard tended to by monks from the Abbey. In the early 18th century it became part of Bath's fashionable social centre.

In 1709, Beau Nash (see page 11) commissioned John Harrison to build the Assembly Rooms on Terrace Walk next to what is Parade Gardens today. The Assembly Room's fashionable visitors sought somewhere to promenade (the act of taking leisurely walks to 'see and be seen'). Consequently Parade Gardens was created, with features such as a summer house, riverside paths and walks, gift shops and lodging houses. Visitors considered the view across the river to the meadows, Bathwick village and the hills beyond to be one of the best in Bath.

The gardens, today open to the public for a small fee, are Grade II listed and boast a number of sculptures, formal and informal lawns and spectacular displays of flowers.

Walking directions *(map on back flap)*

- Turn left out of the Visitor Information Centre, then immediately turn left into York Street.

- Turn left at the end of York Street. Soon after, turn right over two pedestrian crossings to the stone balustrade above Parade Gardens.

- Turn left along Grand Parade, then right over Pulteney Bridge (for more on Pulteney Bridge, see page 14). As you cross the Bridge, you can see Pulteney Weir.

Pulteney Weir

In 1724, the Avon Navigation Company decided transportation on the River Avon would be more economical than carrying goods over steep, badly-maintained roads. So they began work to bypass the river's weirs and shallows between Bath and Bristol with a system of locks and channels, known as lateral canals. In 1727 a barge travelled the length of the Avon between the two cities for the first time. Pulteney Weir marks the upper limit of the navigable river passage between Bristol and Bath.

The project's completion had a profound effect on Bath's life and economy. Cheaper imported materials – essential to Bath's expansion as a tourist centre – became available. These included coal, Welsh iron and slate, Scandinavian timber and wine from Spain. Bath stone was also being shipped out to Bristol, Liverpool, London and Ireland.

Below left The one-hectare (2 ½-acre) Parade Gardens offers beautiful displays – but particularly in summer, when there is three-dimensional carpet bedding

Above A view down the River Avon

Pulteney Bridge
Great Pulteney Street and Bathwick Estate
The Holburne Museum

Pulteney Bridge

In the early 1760s, the 240-hectare (600-acre) Bathwick estate east of the river was entirely rural. Then in 1767 it was inherited by Frances Pulteney (d.1782). Her husband, William Johnstone Pulteney (1729–1805), decided to develop it into a 'New Town' on Frances' behalf.

At the time, Bathwick could only be reached by ferry. So a new bridge to link the estate with the old city was essential to the scheme. From 1769–74, the famous, then-fashionable Scottish architect Robert Adam was brought in to design and build Pulteney Bridge, the only building in Bath designed by him. It is also one of only four bridges in the world with a continuous line of shops running along each side.

Adam's original plan was inspired by Antonio Palladio's rejected classical design for the Rialto Bridge in Venice. However the bridge you see today is now much altered from these original designs. In 1792, a storey was added, the porticos removed and shopfronts changed. After serious flooding in 1800, the north side was radically rebuilt. Further changes followed, including modifications to shop windows and wooden extensions on the north side. Two 20th-century projects partially restored Adam's original design.

The water that would be needed for this new town was to be collected from the slopes beneath Sham Castle (see page 24). Examples of the 20 or more stone spring markers can still be found in those fields.

Great Pulteney Street and Bathwick Estate

This was the 'New Town' William Pulteney decided to develop; Robert Adam even prepared two designs for the proposed estate. However, problems delayed the start of the scheme for almost ten years, until Henrietta Laura Pulteney inherited the estate from her mother in 1782. She commissioned Thomas Baldwin, Bath's chief architect, to produce new plans and building work started in earnest in 1788. The main complex of Laura Place, Great Pulteney Street and part of Bathwick Street was built between 1788 and 1790. Road levels were raised on arched, brick-built vaults to provide level, flood-free streets (you can see this difference by looking at original basement levels of the buildings along Great Pulteney Street).

The unbuilt city

In 1793, following the ruinous wars in America, the Bath banks crashed. Financial chaos and bankruptcy broke out and construction on this

Left Pulteney Bridge, designed by Robert Adam

Opposite above A view of the Holburne Museum

Opposite below Dating from 1793, this map shows the ambitious original plans for the Pulteney Estate, including the unbuilt Great Annandale Street and Frances Square

Walking directions *(map on back flap)*

- Continue straight on to the end of
  Great Pulteney Street. Cross the main
  road at the pedestrian crossings into
  Sydney Place with the Holburne Museum
  (with café and facilities) on your left.
  After 45 yards (40 metres), turn left into
  Sydney Gardens (see page 16).
  Note: during museum opening times,
  you can enter Sydney Gardens through
  the museum grounds.

*For next directions,
turn to page 19*

area ceased, leaving half-finished streets and
abandoned building sites. One, Sunderland
Street, is Britain's shortest street with not even
one house.

In 1795, some building work resumed on the
Bathwick Estate, including terraces in the
Sydney Gardens area. However much of
Thomas Baldwin's estate plan was never
completed. Vast Francis Square, the centre of
the development, and Great Annandale Street,
which would have run parallel to Great Pulteney
Street, remained unfinished. Baldwin's designs
for Sydney Gardens and Sydney House were
never used.

The Holburne Museum (formerly Holburne Museum of Art)

Completed in 1799, this was originally the
three-storey Sydney Hotel. It served as an
entrance to Sydney Gardens, one of Bath's
most popular 18th-century pleasure gardens
(see page 16).

Eating (including Sally Lunn buns, first
recorded as being eaten in Bath), coffee
drinking, newspaper reading and card playing
took place on the ground floor, with dancing on
the first floor above. The Sydney Tap, a public
house accommodating the attendant servants,
was in the basement.

It was also Bath's first public art gallery,
established in 1882. Today it contains fine and
decorative arts, including the collection of
Sir William Holburne (1793–1874). Trustees of the
William Holburne art collection purchased the
building in 1911 and the museum opened in 1916.

The fashionable Georgian spa town

By the late Georgian period, Bath was the premier resort town in England and the best of the country's spas. Its medicinal waters became famous as a cure for gout and other illnesses. The speed of the city's growth was remarkable.

The presence of wealthy visitors with time on their hands sustained the entertainment industry. Many people were employed to provide goods and services for holidaymakers, and the resident population increased.

Much to offer

One of the keys to the city's success was the plethora of opportunities for meeting others. For those who could afford it, Bath offered outdoor and indoor concerts, theatrical entertainments, public breakfasts and dances in the Upper and Lower Assembly Rooms (the former is now National Trust), libraries, bookshops, chocolate and coffee houses, gift shops, gambling and card games. The theatre was considered one of the best in the country. Bath also had the reputation as an unofficial marriage market, a meeting place for the sexes. All this was facilitated by the relaxed attitude to rank encouraged by Beau Nash (see page 11).

Bath's surroundings were another attraction. Visitors came for the sights as well as the company. There were sumptuous buildings like the Circus and Royal Crescent, grand public meeting places, broad new streets and squares, and parks and gardens for promenading and entertainment in fine weather. There were the views from Bath out to the green hills and skyline beyond and, for those who explored the immediate countryside on foot, horseback or by carriage, the surrounding countryside offered fresh air and glorious panoramas. Bath became a mecca for health and leisure, highly appealing to both young and old.

Sydney Gardens

Opened in 1795 and designed by Charles Harcourt Masters, Sydney Gardens was the largest pleasure garden in the country outside London and the most successful in Bath. Like other 18th-century pleasure gardens, they were a commercial enterprise designed to amuse and delight. In return for an entrance fee, a rich variety of entertainment was available, including public breakfasts, evening promenades and gala nights of music, illuminations and fireworks. Throughout the day you could eat, drink and meet others.

Originally, the gardens included two bowling greens, two swings, unusual trees and shrubs, a sham castle, grotto and refreshment facilities. Later, a large labyrinth was added with a Merlin Mechanical Swing, which cost 6d. Swinging was not permitted on Sundays.

Above The Sydney Hotel depicted by H. S. Storer in 1818 – the hotel is now the Holburne Museum

Opposite The Jane Austen festival, taking place in the Bath Assembly Rooms

Jane Austen and Bath

A microcosm of Georgian society, Bath offered novelist Jane Austen useful material. Her familiarity with the city and its social life enriches the accounts of the city's residents, visitors, streets and buildings that appear in her two 'Bath' novels, *Northanger Abbey* and *Persuasion*. Both were published posthumously, but not long after Austen's death in 1817. It appears she wasn't a huge fan of Bath's social life herself, though: 'We are to have a tiny party here tonight; I hate tiny parties – they force one into constant exertion,' she wrote to her cousin Cassandra in May 1801.

Austen came to the city on a number of occasions: first in November 1797, when she stayed with a well-off aunt and uncle, then in May 1799 she stayed with her wealthiest brother and his family in Queen Square. In 1801, following her father's retirement, she moved with her parents to 4 Sydney Place. In 1805, she and her mother lived in Gay Street. In 1806 she lived briefly in Trim Street, before leaving Bath for good in the summer.

Industrial growth

In the early 19th century, Bath continued to develop from a high-class seasonal resort for visitors into a place of permanent residence for the middle and upper classes. At the same time, the city became increasingly industrial and commercial.

The building industry and stone quarrying continued to expand. Steam-powered production of beer, soap, glass and textiles was established. Retailing and commerce grew. Traditional craft industries such as cabinet making, shoemaking, tailoring and coach construction expanded. New industries of printing, bookbinding, engineering and machine making were introduced. Stothert and Pitt, originally an ironmongery business, grew into a mechanical engineering company, internationally famous for the manufacture of dockside cranes, possibly including the – still working – steam-powered crane in Bristol's harbour. In 1845, Sir Isaac Pitman, who pioneered shorthand, established a major printing and publishing company which became widely known for its shorthand, educational and commercial books. In the nearby village of Bathampton, Plasticine, invented by William Harbutt, was manufactured on a commercial scale from 1900.

The transport boom

This industrial and commercial growth was partly the result of developments in local transport, which created links between Bath firms and previously untapped national markets.

The Kennet and Avon Canal, which opened in 1810, made it possible to transport goods to London in four days. This transportation time decreased to a matter of hours when the Great Western Railway opened in 1841. By the end of the 19th century, Bath had become a small-scale industrial city. At the same time, it had firmly established its dominant image as a genteel place of permanent residence with many rich cultural traditions, including its architectural heritage.

The Kennet and Avon Canal

The 57-mile-long Kennet and Avon Canal created a direct water connection between Bath and London. Designed by John Rennie, it was joined near Monkton Combe by the Somerset Coal Canal which brought coal from North Somerset. The arrival of this utilitarian thoroughfare passing through the middle of fashionable Bath caused no small amount of controversy at the time and the beautiful designs of the wrought iron bridges that we see today were built in an effort to mollify local feeling.

Although successful in the early part of the 19th century, the canal was later superseded and purchased by the Great Western Railway and gradually fell into disuse. It was abandoned in 1952, restored in stages, and fully reopened in 1990, largely through the work of volunteers. Today barges once more ply the canal, both for holidaymaking and as longer-term residences.

Walking directions *(map on back flap)*

- Follow the tarmac path towards a stone 'temple' to meet a wide tarmac path and turn right, over the railway bridge. Immediately before the next bridge (over the canal), turn right beneath a large plane tree. After 11 yards (10m), go through a white iron gateway on the left, on to the canal towpath, and turn right. Follow the towpath through the tunnel and up a ramp to cross the canal. Turn right to continue on the towpath. At the boat basin, go up the cobbled ramp and cross the road (Bathwick Hill). Turn right over the bridge, then a sharp left by the supermarket, down steep steps to continue right along the towpath.

- At lock 13, cross the canal footbridge, then go up the slope and steps to Sydney Buildings. Cross the road and walk up two flights of steps, then continue 330 yards (300m) on the path beside Bathwick Fields (for more on Bathwick Fields, see page 20). Pass two kissing gates until you reach the end of the black railings and a wooden bench in the field on your right, with a magnificent view to reward your efforts.

Opposite The Kennet and Avon Canal

Left Bristol's Fairburn crane, created by the Bath-based Stothert and Pitt company. It is the only surviving example of a steam-powered Fairburn crane

Taking the air

Enjoying exercise and fresh air played an important part in the social life of visitors to Georgian Bath.

Promenading in the city's public walks and pleasure gardens was primarily a social activity, but was also considered a means to good health. Seeking health and pleasure in the surrounding countryside, whether on horseback, on foot or in coaches, was an important part of a visitor's social ritual.

Routes to the view

Riders and carriages often crowded the picturesque routes along the Avon valley, particularly the Upper and Lower Bristol roads. Steeper journeys to Claverton and Lansdown were also popular. For more serious exercise, people walked the popular footpaths along the river, across the fields to Weston and Bathampton, or up the slopes to Claverton Down.

Many of these routes offered wonderful views. Beechen Cliff's was considered outstanding, and it was thought attractive from a distance too: in *Northanger Abbey*, Jane Austen describes it as 'that noble hill whose beautiful verdure and hanging coppice render it so striking an object from almost every opening in Bath'. Widcombe Hill and its neighbourhood were thought to offer the best views to the east; artists produced numerous illustrations from the summit above Smallcombe Wood (see page 46).

'And what fine Air do the Invalids breath in upon them? I will venture to say, that thirty different Rides, each sufficient for a Morning's Airing…may be found about BATH, as conducive to the Health and Pleasure of Mankind in general, as can be met with in ten Times the Space of Ground in any other Country.'

John Wood the Elder, *An Essay Towards a Description of Bath*, 1749

Bathwick Hill

Until the early 19th century, the road that is now Bathwick Hill was just a field with a pathway through to Claverton Down. The creation of the road made it much easier to reach a beauty spot near its summit that looked out over Smallcombe Wood and the area we now know as Bathwick Fields, and offered fine views over the city and beyond.

In 1984 these fields were purchased by the National Trust following a generous donation

from the Council and funds raised from grants and public appeals.

North Parade Bridge

Together with South Parade, Pierrepoint Street and Duke Street, North Parade is part of a single square-shaped design created by John Wood the Elder in 1738. The scheme was originally intended to extend further south as a 'Royal Forum', but the idea was eventually abandoned. Wood's scheme was completed to a modified design in 1748.

In 1836 bridge engineer William Tierney Clark built North Parade Bridge as an extension of North Parade across the river. The original bridge was made of cast iron on stone piers with lodges and staircases. This was rebuilt in 1936 and the cast iron re-faced with stone.

Walking directions *(map on back flap)*

- Just past the end of the field, turn right down a narrow footpath, with a hedge on the right. Pass the gateway on the right. Shortly after, turn right over a small footbridge and stile in the hedgerow.

- Walk straight across the field and through two kissing gates in close succession (into and out of Richens Orchard – see page 49 for more information on the Orchard). After the second gate, turn left, keeping the field boundary on the left. Go through the kissing gate adjacent to the wide gateway.

- From the gateway, continue straight ahead for 100 yards (90m) to a dip in the field, then left downhill to a kissing gate, on to Sydney Buildings road, and turn right. Shortly after turn left, retrace the route back to the canal tow path, and turn right. After 90 yards (80m), turn left on to footpath going downhill. Continue straight, past the end of the cul-de-sac, until reaching Pulteney Road beneath the railway bridge. Cross straight over at the pedestrian crossing on to North Bridge.

- Continue along North Parade until the junction with Pierrepoint Street. Cross straight over on to Terrace Walk. Shortly after, turn left into York Street, which leads you back to the Visitor Information Centre.

Above Buttercups blooming in Bathwick Fields

Below Bathwick Fields, with the city of Bath just visible in the distance

The Bath Skyline Walk

This six-mile circular walk takes you through fields and woodlands, and over the sites of ancient settlements and quarries that once delivered Bath stone to the city.

The view from North Road over Bath

Where to start

The recommended starting point is Cleveland Walk, on the opposite side of the road to the National Trust bus stop on Bathwick Hill, and the order of this guidebook reflects this route. However you might also choose to begin at the Bath Cats & Dogs Home (page 33) or the Woodland Play Area on Claverton Down (page 41).

Things to note

- Paths may be muddy and are steep in places, so we recommend sturdy footwear
- Cattle and sheep graze meadows throughout the walk – please keep dogs under effective control and clear up after them
- You will cross some stiles and gates
- If you'd like to avoid the steep hills, there are lots of footpaths that detour from the route shown in the map at the front of this guide; these cross level ground

How to get here

By car: There are no National Trust car parks on the Skyline, but there are frequent bus services from the city centre.

By foot: The walk is about ¾ mile (1.2km) from the city centre – proceed up Bathwick Hill and join the walk at point 1, the junction with Cleveland Walk. You could also do the 'Walk to the View', which leads to Bathwick Fields (see pages 12–21).

By bus: Take the City Sightseeing tour bus from Bath Spa railway station and alight at stops 'M' or 'N' for Claverton Down and the Woodland Play Area. Alternatively, take buses 'U1' or 'U18', City Centre to Bath University, and alight at Cleveland Walk. The buses leave opposite the bus station.

By train: Bath Spa station is about a one-mile (1.6km) walk from Bathwick Fields.

Walking directions *(map on front flap)*

1. Start the walk at the National Trust Bus Stop on Bathwick Hill with Bathwick Fields behind you. The walk begins with a short residential section before becoming a countryside walk. Cross the road (Bathwick Hill) to Cleveland Walk opposite the bus stop. Continue along Cleveland Walk past large houses for approximately ¼ mile (400m) until you reach a narrow footpath between two high walls on the right opposite Sham Castle Lane. Follow the steep path and go up steps at the end to meet North Road. Turn right and continue up to a metal kissing gate on the opposite side of the road by a large green 'Sham Castle Down' sign. Carefully cross the road, go up the concrete steps and through the kissing gate.

2. Continue up the wooden steps and steep uphill path through a field with trees on both sides. Go through a metal kissing gate on to a small road (Golf Course Road) at the top of the hill where you will enjoy a beautiful view of the city behind you.

At this point, we recommend going on a very short detour to see Sham Castle – directions for this are on page 25.

If you would prefer to continue on the Skyline route, turn to page 27.

Sham Castle

Sham Castle stands on the crest of the hill on Bathampton Down, facing the city. However this is not a real castle, but an ornamental folly.

Sham Castle, a Grade II-listed building, is one of three such follies overlooking the city (the others are Beckford's Tower on Lansdown Hill and Brown's Folly near Bathford). It can be seen from the city centre, including at night, when it's illuminated.

The idea for the folly took root in 1755 when William Pitt, the local MP, sought to commission a 'Gothick object' for Ralph Allen from Sanderson Miller. Miller was renowned in the area for his extensive reworking of many of Lacock Abbey's Tudor features in the Gothick style.

A site was chosen – a building that was on the edge of Bathampton Pillow Mounds known as Warren House or Anstey Lodge. Work was carried out by Richard Jones, Allen's Clerk of Works, and completed in 1762.

Originally painted in white and with a tree-lined backdrop, the castle would have been a striking feature on the city's horizon. It is also an excellent example of the many crenelated 'eye-catchers' that were popular features of English landscaped gardens in the 18th century. It's clear the castle was only supposed to be seen from one side, however: the back is completely flat.

Opposite The front of Sham Castle

Right A detail on the side of Sham Castle

Far right Sanderson Miller c.1750, thought to have been painted by Thomas Hudson

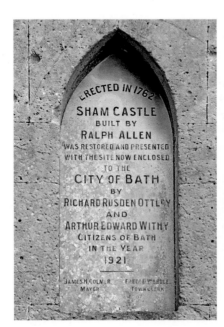

'[the castle and plantation] appear pleasing objects, not only from almost every part of the city, but through a great extent of the county westward to the other side of the Severn, the light colour of the stone forming a conspicuous contrast with the deep mass of shade from the grove close behind it.'

Reverend Collinson, 1791

Why was it constructed?

It has traditionally been thought that Ralph Allen built Sham Castle to 'improve the prospect' from his city townhouse. But by the time the castle was built in 1762, he was no longer resident there and other buildings such as the Parade Coffee House would have restricted the view. Instead, he may have built Sham as a gift to the people of the city or to advertise the excellent qualities of his Bath stone as a building material.

Walking directions *(map on front flap)*

To reach Sham Castle, cross over the small road and go up the path past a small stone building on your right. Continue up through the wood as the path bends to the right until you reach a bench in front of Sham Castle. Return to the main route by going back the same way you came.

Bathwick Wood and Bathampton Down

Today, much of Bathampton Down is the site of Bath Golf Club, which was established in 1880. But it's likely that, thousands of years ago, there was a settlement here.

Bathwick Wood

Venture here in spring, and you might stumble across patches of bluebells, or detect the scent of wild garlic in the air. Later in the year, in autumn, the trees put on a fiery display.

There's also plenty of archaeological and historical intrigue. The building platforms and quarries of Bathwick Wood probably date to Roman times; certainly the many finds of Roman coins and pottery fragments in the area suggest that this was indeed an important site during the Roman occupation. If Roman in origin, these extensively worked quarries would be of international importance for their rarity. Perhaps they were the property of a local villa owner or part of an imperial estate managed for the Emperor.

Below **Bathwick Wood**

Opposite above **The pillow mounds on Bathampton Down**

Opposite below left **Brown's Folly at Farleigh Down, Bathford, which can be seen from the Skyline walk**

Opposite below right **A view of Little Solsbury Hill**

The long mounds on the right as you cross Bathampton Down are known as pillow mounds: artificial warrens created in medieval times, in this case by Bishop William Button, to farm rabbits.

Bathampton Down

The Bathampton Down enclosure was once thought to be a hill fort, but at 30 hectares (74 acres), it's too large for this to have been the case.

It's also probably too old; excavations in the 1960s found a wide shallow ditch and rampart marking the Camp's boundary which contained late Bronze Age to early Iron Age pottery from c.800–500BC and most hillforts were not established until after 500BC.

Pottery found on Trust land near Sham Castle (see page 24) is from a similar date, suggesting there was a farm here around the same time that Bathampton Camp was being used. It's thought the Camp formed a large livestock enclosure used to keep grazing animals secure. We think the whole area was divided up as arable fields in the later Iron Age, and continued to be used throughout the Roman period.

For more about Bathampton Down, turn to page 30.

Walking directions *(map on front flap)*

③ From the metal kissing gate turn left and walk past a bench, keeping the view of Bath to your left and immediately take the path into the woodland (Bathwick Wood) down a short flight of wooden steps. Go along the woodland path continuing all the way through. Ignore a metal kissing gate on the left and instead continue along the path which almost immediately bends to the right up a rocky path. Continue along path up a steep slope. Continue uphill through the woodland to a metal kissing gate at the top.

④ Go through the kissing gate and turn left on to the track through a field, keeping the woods to your left and you will soon see a golf course to your right. Continue past a metal kissing gate on the left. Where the track runs right to the radio masts, continue straight on to the field. Follow the path indicated by the waymarker and continue across the middle of the field keeping to the same level. Other footpaths cross the field heading in the same direction and also end at the same point, but aim to keep to the path on the left. After crossing a line of small trees, and about 165 yards (150m) before you reach Bathampton Wood, the view to your left begins to open up showing Little Solsbury Hill to the left behind you and Brown's Folly (a folly of a tower built in 1848) to the left ahead. (Discover more about Little Solsbury Hill on page 28.) Walk down a short slope that bears left, turn right into the wood (Bathampton Wood), going over a wooden stile.

Little Solsbury Hill

Made famous by Peter Gabriel's popular song in the 1970s, this hill site, which you can see as you cross Bathampton Down (and access from Batheaston), has been inhabited for a thousand years.

Although stray finds can be dated to the later Neolithic (2600–2300BC) and Bronze Age (2300–700BC), the area's key feature is the eight-hectare (eighteen-acre) hill fort, a defended settlement occupied over two thousand years ago.

It is not part of the Bath Skyline walk, but you will spot it from this section of the route – and the views from it make it worth a separate trip to the countryside.

Life on the fort

This area was once crammed with Iron Age round houses and people. With a near-level hill top, clear views in all directions and protected by steep slopes, it's easy to see why this made the perfect location for a fort.

In the 1950s, excavations concluded the fort was probably occupied in the earlier Iron Age, c.300BC, but had been abandoned at least one hundred years before the Roman army conquered the area in c.AD44. It was eventually surrounded by a carefully constructed stone-faced rampart with an entrance on the north-west. Within this resided a warrior farmer community who lived in round houses, each made of a ring of timber posts infilled with mud and woven branches and a thatched conical roof. A 2012 survey by the Bath and Camerton Archaeological Society revealed the sites of over fifty such round houses here, each surrounded by a distinctive circular drainage ditch.

The community would have grazed cattle and sheep (bones from both were discovered during the 1950s digs). A bridle bit suggests that wealthier inhabitants rode horses. Flour was produced from harvested grain, using quern-stones discovered here in the 1950s. Two decorated weaving combs show that clothing was made, while the uncovering of two spearheads and sling stones demonstrated that the inhabitants were armed and ready to defend their homes.

The 1950s digs also showed that the earliest houses were built before the hill top was defended. The first rampart was pulled down, perhaps after an attack, and then another wall was constructed, associated with a new form of pottery. Does this suggest invaders and, if so, what happened to the original Solsbury dwellers? Or did they just buy some more fashionable pottery and rebuild their defences?

Opposite An aerial view of Little Solsbury Hill

Left Spearpoints and weaving combs discovered on Little Solsbury Hill during the excavations in the 1950s

Medieval farmers to modern times

Many centuries later, Little Solsbury's abandoned earthworks were being ploughed by medieval farmers, who trudged up and down their strip farming system behind ox teams. The narrow fields were marked by mere stones, each engraved with an allotment holder's initials. They continued to be ploughed right up to the 19th century. By this time the surrounding hill slopes were being quarried for limestone; it was in these quarries that the earliest recorded archaeological discoveries were made.

Quarrying continued right up until the 1960s, and the summit similarly reflected this history of more intensive management, with barley being grown until 1950. Today the area is accessible to all, with the site designated as common land.

How to get here

There is no parking at the top of the hill, but there is a car park in Batheaston village at its foot. Following Solsbury Lane, the walk up from the village is 1 2/5 miles (2km) long, quite steep and takes about 45 minutes.

Ralph Allen at Bathampton Down

During the 1700s, Ralph Allen owned much of this area, including the Manor, and the quarries that changed the face of Bath.

The quarries

As is particularly clear from the Skyline, much of Bath is built from a distinctive, honey-yellow stone. Known as 'Bath stone', this was quarried from mines at Combe Down and Bathampton Down.

Although the Romans were known to have used the stone for important fortifications, it was in the 18th century, from around 1730, that its use really took off. This was mostly thanks to Ralph Allen, who had bought the land here a few years earlier; the tramways and cart-roads he created to transport the stone can still be seen in some places, such as Bathampton Wood. His stone rebuilt much of Bath and was used elsewhere in the UK too, including at Bristol Cathedral and Tyntesfield, near Bristol (also National Trust).

Ralph Allen died in 1764 and his wife two years later; the estate passed to his niece Gertrude Warburton and her husband. In 1769, due to financial pressures from having to meet bequests in Allan's will, Gertrude decided to leave the estate, sell off the contents and lease Prior Park mansion. In the 19th century, the stone was used to relay the Kennet and Avon Canal and an incline was constructed to cover the 800-yard (730-metre) distance between the quarries and Canal. In 1810, the Canal Company also used the stone to construct docks, but soon found that all the best material had already been used up.

Reminders of the work that took place here can be seen throughout the golf course: a disused quarry creates a hazard in front of the tees for the 14th hole, while throughout are bomb-like craters, left over from surface quarrying. The 6.22 hectares (15.37 acres) of mine are now a designated Site of Special Scientific Interest (SSSI) due to their resident greater and lesser horseshoe bat population.

Above A panoramic view of the Skyline from Bathampton Down

Bathampton Manor

Bathampton Down was part of the estate of Bathampton Manor, on the banks of the Avon. This was probably where Ralph Allen's second wife, Elizabeth, spent all her life until she married Allen in 1737. Allen acquired the (relatively) modest manor from Elizabeth's brother five years later but he probably never lived here, preferring Prior Park (see page 42).

As well as the house and Down, the almost 400-hectare (985-acre) estate included Bathampton Warren, a poorhouse, parsonage and many farms. In the 1750s, Allen added tree-lined avenues to the estate and a pleasure ground with ornamental features along the riverside. After his death, the house passed to his nephew, Philip, and was enlarged. It remained a residence for Allen's descendants until it was sold in 1921. The Manor – which is part of Bathwick – has since been converted into a care home.

Walking directions *(map on front flap)*

5 Go along the winding and rocky path through the woods until reaching a junction up a short slope where the old tramway with remnant footings crosses your path. Don't follow the tramway path that goes downhill, go straight across, past large rocks on both sides and up a short slope between two trees where the path splits again. Take the wider path in the middle, which goes past a large rocky cliff on the right. Keep to the higher path, which goes over uneven and rocky surfaces; take care where the path crosses a small rocky gap with a drop to the left. Ignore any smaller paths leading down the hill to your left. The path ascends gently to a large Y junction; here bear left on the path. After a short distance you will reach a metal kissing gate.

Bathampton Wood to Bushey Norwood

**Bushey Norwood
in winter**

Walking directions *(map on front flap)*

6 Exit Bathampton Wood through the kissing gate into a very large open field (Bushey Norwood – turn to page 34 for more information about this area). Continue through the field keeping the fence and woods on your left. At the end of the field, go through a gate in the stone wall and bear right. Cross the field leaving the stone wall and fence to your right until reaching a gate. Go through the gate and turn left along the track. Note the pedestrian entrance to the American Museum in Britain on the left where facilities and a café are available (opening times and admission fees apply). Turn right before reaching the metal gates by the road and instead go through a wooden gate on to University of Bath land. Ignore the first turn on the right and at the Y junction take the left path leading to a stone stile over the wall (next to a large tree). Go over the stile and turn right on to the road (Claverton Hill, becoming The Avenue further along). Continue for 110 yards (100m) along the road, going carefully as there is no footpath. Turn left on to a public footpath between a gap in a stone wall just before Bath Cats & Dogs Home. Continue along the path keeping the sports fields on your left. Continue along the narrow footpath at the end until reaching the road (Claverton Down Road). Go left along the road for roughly 44 yards (40m) then carefully cross over this busy road to the small lay-by car park.

For next directions, turn to page 37

Right The Dry Arch that took the tramway from Bathampton Down across the Warminster Road to the Kennet and Avon Canal

Bushey Norwood

Walking south across Bushey Norwood field, away from Bathampton Wood, you'll notice undulations in the grass. These are the remains of an ancient farm – the walls that would once have enclosed livestock – and are one of a number that would have been located across the Bath Skyline landscape 2–4,000 years ago.

In 1888, while riding his horse, Colonel Henry Skrine – then owner of the estate – spotted a wall sticking out of the grass on the east of the fields. He asked his men to investigate. Beneath the turf, they found a wall surviving almost a metre high. The Colonel concluded that it must have once enclosed a cluster of round houses like ones he had seen in Cornwall, and had probably been occupied by a group of related families and their store houses. He also mentions finding ancient pottery, meat bones, stone tools and fragments of querns, used for grinding corn into flour.

There were also flints; rarely used in the Iron Age, their presence suggests this site pre-dates the hill fort settlement at Little Solsbury Hill (see page 28). So Bushey's walled enclosure may date to the later Bronze Age (about 1200–700BC), although we cannot be certain without seeing the Colonel's finds or excavating the site ourselves. The field system would have continued to be used and adapted throughout the Iron Age and Roman periods.

The earthworks are long banks forming small field enclosures. They have become grass-covered over time but underneath they are made of stone fragments. These boundary walls were probably piled up from field clearance to separate good soil from rock and make ploughing easier.

Life at Bushey Norwood

The families living here would have ploughed the small fields and grown mainly wheat or barley, which they would have made into porridge, bread or beer. They would have kept dogs as pets and for herding and security. They reared livestock for food, dining on mutton, beef and occasionally pork, and their diets were supplemented by gathering and storing seasonal plants such as berries, leaves and roots.

The other Skyline farms

Similar groups of ancient fields can be found across the Bath Skyline. The most extensive can be seen on the golf course on Bathampton Down (see page 27), but Rainbow Wood Farm – a tenanted National Trust Farm on Claverton Down – also has some good surviving remains. Here, the curving field boundary shapes change to straight lines and suggest a Roman modification of the farming system. By this time the wealthier farmers on the Bath Skyline had stopped living in round houses and now occupied rectangular stone buildings.

Flora and fauna

Bushey Norwood is a great spot on the Skyline to birdwatch. In winter, the fields here, as well as at the golf course, attract flocks of fieldfares, meadow pipits, redwings and starlings, together with common gulls, and sometimes lapwings and even golden plovers.

Top left Fieldfares start to arrive in the UK from October. They tend to stay until March or possibly April

Bottom left Although starlings appear black from a distance, up close they are glossy with a sheen of purples and greens

Top right Meadow pipits tend to be found in open country

Bottom right Golden plovers typically stand upright and run in short bursts

Claverton Down

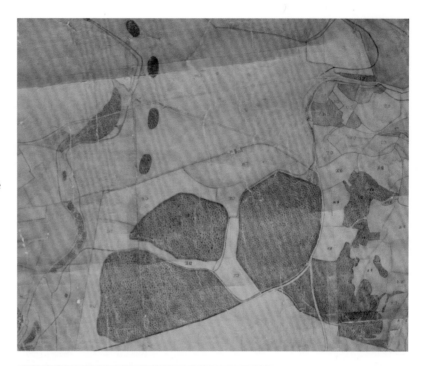

As you reach Claverton Down, you are crossing the boundary into a former medieval deer park, of which the origins date back to the days of William the Conquerer.

'The Great Park'

In 1091, Bishop John Villula of Tours (see page 10) was granted the city of Bath and Abbey. At the same time, the bishop was given a licence to make a deer park or warren in the monastery lands, which covered the southern parts of Claverton Down and extended to the upper reaches of Widcombe. The area was sometimes known as 'The Great Park' and remnants of the medieval boundary walls still survive along Hanginglands Lane and below Rainbow Wood.

In 1223, part of the Bishop's holdings, including the western half of the deer park, were transferred to the prior of Bath Abbey. Subsequently, a Bishop's Park and Prior's Park were created; the divisions between the two followed the same boundary wall that still sits between the parishes of Claverton (once the bishop's side) and Widcombe (which now runs alongside the Combe down to the University cycle track). We think the priors used their side for hunting with hawks, until the dissolution of the monasteries in the 16th century. Later, in the 17th century, the land was enclosed and used for agriculture.

What was a deer park?
In medieval and early modern England, deer parks were granted by the king. In them, wealthy men were allowed to hunt the beasts of the forest such as red, fallow and roe deer, and wild boar. Such activities were usually the exclusive preserve of royalty.

Above Detail from Ralph Allen's 1762 estate map showing Claverton Down to the north and west of Brassnocker Hill. Curiously, this shows that the areas that were once woodland have, over the intervening 250 years, changed to be mostly fields and vice versa

Allen at Claverton Down

From 1726, Ralph Allen started to purchase land in the area for his estate. Between 1726 and 1728, he bought land in Widcombe and Monkton Combe, including the stone quarrying rights on Combe Down and parts of the grounds of the old Prior's Park. In 1742 he bought the manor and lordship of Bathampton, including Bathampton Down and Bathampton Warren, from his brother-in-law, Charles Holder. In 1758, this was followed by Claverton Manor, which also comprised Claverton Down.

By the time of his death in 1764, Allen's estate – which covered more than 1,200 hectares (3,000 acres) – stretched across the downs to the south of Bath and down to the river Avon, almost without interruption. To the west lay Combe Down and Odd Down, to the east Claverton Down and Bathampton Down. Allen had restored the medieval park to single ownership.

Claverton Manor

When Allen purchased Claverton Manor, the estate comprised 526 hectares (1,300 acres) of downland, hillside and a valley bordering the River Avon. Although he continued to live at Prior Park (see pages 42–5) the Manor, which was small and rural, provided Allen with a welcome retreat from his busy public life in Bath. He often entertained his friends here and linked it to Prior Park by building a tree-lined avenue across the downs.

This manor wasn't the building that now contains the American Museum in Britain, but an old Jacobean mansion in Claverton village, probably designed by John of Padua in the late 16th century. The estate also included a church, extensive lands and 'the best vineyard' in all England (John Aubrey, *Natural History of Wiltshire*, 1656–91). In 1819–20, long after Allen and his descendants had left, the old manor was replaced with the present building, which is further up the slope of Claverton Down. This became the American Museum in Britain in 1961.

Walking directions *(map on front flap)*

⑦ Go through the wooden gate at the left of the lay-by, follow the path around the field edge and you will see a farm, called Rainbow Wood Farm, to your right. At this point you have entered the area known as Claverton Down. Continue for a total of 875 yards (800m) along the main path, through a number of wooden gates, until reaching woodland on your right.

For next directions, turn to page 41

Above **The American Museum in Britain, formerly Claverton Manor**

Claverton Down: the duels and the races

In the early 1720s, Claverton Down was a popular venue for horse-racing.

In 1723, Bath Corporation took a lease on the area to allow the public, especially Bath's wealthy visitors, to ride and race there. Racing on Claverton Down is first recorded in the official *Racing Calendar* in 1728 (although we know racing was taking place informally at least seven years beforehand). That year, 'Smiling Ball' won his owner a prize of 50 guineas by racing against three other horses and coming in first in each of three heats. In 1740, the races and associated sideshows lapsed after Parliament passed an Act 'to restrain and prevent the excessive increase of Horse Races', but two-day racing events returned in 1744. Two-day meetings were also staged from 1756–8. Then in 1758, Ralph Allen bought Claverton Manor; racing ceased after the following year's meeting.

When racing was allowed on his land, Allen was not a fan of the accompanying dogs. 'If any person hath a Dog, that he wishes to be shot or hanged, if he will produce him on the Down his Wish shall be gratify'd,' he 'advised'.

'And hey for the Race on Clarton-Down [sic]'

The Pleasures of Bath, 1721

Days at the races

In 1770, six years after Ralph Allen had died, events resumed. The golden age of horse-racing at Claverton had begun.

A grandstand with numbered seating and a gallery was provided near the Down House, now Rainbow Wood Farm. Also near the house were stables to provide for an excellent field of thoroughbreds for three days of racing. From 1771, regular four-day racing events took place. Landlords, including the host of the 'Horse and Jockey' on Claverton Down, competed for the right to set up drinking booths on the racecourse. Bath accommodated all the extra visitors to the early autumn meetings, putting on nightly performances at the theatre and balls at the Upper Assembly Rooms. Huge numbers visited the city for the races: on just one day in 1777, Claverton Down entertained 800 carriages and 20,000 visitors on foot and horseback.

The last racing days

The popularity of the races appeared to decline the following year. On the last day of the meeting, they had zero, one and two runners only – although this was partly due to the condition of the course. In 1784, organised racing was moved to a new course at Lansdown, to the north of the city, where it still takes place today.

However, the racecourse was still used by residents and visitors, who visited to 'take the air' on horseback and in carriages.

Above The road over Brassknocker Hill, depicted by Jean Claude Nattes

The duel of Claverton Down

In the 18th century, parts of Claverton Down were well known for duelling and highway robberies, especially at the top of Brassknocker Hill. One such fierce duel took place in November 1778, contested between Irishman Count Rice and the Viscount du Barry – the husband of Madame du Barry, Louis XIV of France's mistress. Following a dispute over a game of cards, the men took to the hills, along with a coach and their 'seconds', each armed with a brace of pistols and sword.

The Viscount's opening shot hit Rice in the thigh; the Count retaliated with a shot to du Barry's chest. Although the duel continued for a little time after, it was this shot that proved to be the fatal blow. Du Barry asked to be spared and, moments after Rice acquiesced, the Viscount died. His body remained on Claverton Down until the following day, and is now buried in St Nicholas Church, Bathampton. Rice was sentenced for murder, but – perhaps due to his good standing and contacts in Bath – was acquitted, the verdict manslaughter.

Bath, Nov. 23, 1778.

The following is an authentic account of the affair that happened at Bath between Count Rice and Viscount du Barry.

On Tuesday last, the 17th instant, Count Rice and Viscount du Barry, being together in the latter's house, a question arose between them, about which they disagreed; and in the heat of the dispute, upon an assertion of Count Rice, Viscount du Barry said, 'Cela n'est pas vrai:' to which Count Rice immediately observed, 'You do not probably observe the idea that expression conveys in the language you speak in, and it admits but of one very disagreeable interpretation; upon which the other replied, 'You may interpret it as you please.'. This ungentleman-like treatment having provoked the resentment of Count Rice, and Viscount du Barry offering no satisfaction, they immediately sent for seconds, who did not quit them till they got to Calverton Down, where they remained together, with a Surgeon, till day-light, when they took the field, each armed with two pistols and a sword. The ground being marked out by the seconds, the Viscount du Barry fired first, and lodged a ball in Count Rice's thigh, which penetrated as far as the bone; Count Rice fired his pistol and wounded the Viscount in the breast. He went back two or three steps, then came forward again, and both, at the same time, presented their pistols to each other; the pistols flashed together in the pan, though one only was discharged. Then they threw away their pistols, and took to their swords; when Count Rice had advanced within a few yards of the Viscount, he saw him fall upon his rump, and heard him cry out, 'je vous demande la vie,' [I ask you for my life]; to which Count Rice answered, 'je vous la donne,' [take it;] but in a few seconds the Viscount fell back, and expired. Count Rice was brought with difficulty to Bath, being dangerously wounded, though in a fair way of recovery.

Tha Coroner's Inquest sat on the Viscount's body last Saturday, and after a mature examination of the witnesses, and the Viscount's servants, brought in their verdict manslaughter.

WILLIAM BRERETON, M. C.

Monument Field
Rainbow Wood

Monument near Prior Park, Bath.
Erected by Bishop Warburton to the Memory of his predecessor at Prior Park, Ralph Allen, who died in 1764.

'One of the neatest gothic piles'

Richard Jones, Allen's clerk of works talking about The Lodge

Monument Field

Lying south-east of Prior Park mansion, this is now a school playing field. It takes its name from a memorial to Ralph Allen that was once situated here.

The Lodge and the Monument

When Ralph Allen obtained the lawns to the east of Prior Park mansion in 1750, he also acquired a large Gothic building known as The Lodge. This had existed in the late 16th century, perhaps developed from a medieval lodge, which would have either been used as a shelter for a hunting party, or housing for a custodian during other periods. There was also an impressive tower in front of the building that would have had excellent views of the surrounding countryside.

Following Allen's death, his niece, Gertrude, inherited the estate and demolished part of The Lodge. Her husband, Bishop Warburton, replaced it with a monument to Allen, which preserved many of the features of the original building, including the front wall and two-storey round tower with its cone-shaped roof. Above the door was a Latin inscription, which translated as: 'You who value true and uncomplicated goodness, venerate this stone, Sacred to the memory of a splendid man, Ralph Allen.'

The Monument, sometimes known as Bishop Warburton's Tower, fell into disrepair during the 19th century and was finally demolished in 1953.

Rainbow Wood *(see direction 9)*

Situated to the east of Prior Park, Rainbow Wood's name is thought to have originated from its bow-like shape and the varied autumn colours produced by the cleverly constructed planting scheme. From Allen's estate maps, it appears the area was newly planted in about 1740, although some medieval woodland might have been there in Allen's day.

Originally the woodland may have consisted of three distinct bands of trees, 'one of pines; one of cedars; one of Scotch firs, in the like semi-circular order' (Samuel Richardson, *The History of Sir Charles Grandison*, 1753).

Walking directions *(map on front flap)*

8 Turn right into the woodland, follow the main path which passes through the Woodland Play Area (see page 53) and through a gap in a stone wall. Continue for 3/5 mile (1km) along the path through woodland until you reach a wooden gate in the stone wall. Cross straight over a cycle track and continue round the outside of the playing field, keeping it to your right. This playing field was once Monument Field (see page opposite). After following the field boundary for 440 yards (400m), bear left down a rocky slope through trees (ignoring the wooden stile straight ahead).

Opposite **Ralph Allen's Monument on Monument Fields** *c.*1915

Left **Anthills at sunrise**

Prior Park

In 1728, Ralph Allen commissioned John Wood the Elder to produce designs for a new house that would demonstrate the high quality of the stone from his nearby quarry.

Building began about five years later, but Wood was dismissed after a quarrel with Allen over changes to his design made by Richard Jones, Allen's clerk of works. Some time before 1950, Jones took over and work on the house was completed after Wood's death in 1754.

The Landscape Garden was constructed in three phases between 1734 and c.1764 and features one of the Bath's most iconic landmarks – the Palladian Bridge, one of only four in the world. Other features included a grotto, a serpentine river crossed by a sham bridge, a Gothic temple, a pineapple house, and a thatched cottage. The initial phase had input from Wood and Alexander Pope.

Above The Palladian Bridge at Prior Park

Opposite An oil painting of 'Capability' Brown c.1770–5, after Sir Nathaniel Dance-Holland

After Allen

Following the deaths of Allen and his wife in 1764 and 1766 respectively, the estate had a series of owners. It was a seminary (an institution for education in theology) which later suffered a serious fire, and housed a Roman Catholic Grammar School, the army during the First World War and a series of tenants. Then in 1921 the Christian Brothers took it over and, three years later, founded a boys' boarding school. A school has occupied the house ever since; it's now a mixed public school for day and boarding students.

In 1993, 11 hectares (27 acres) of the park and pleasure grounds were acquired by the National Trust, and have seen a detailed restoration programme to the Palladian Bridge, lakes, dams and gardens. These are open to the public (entrance fees apply).

Walking directions *(map on front flap)*

9 Turn right and pass through stone pillars. Continue along the path (called The Balcony) with trees to your right (known as Rainbow Wood, see page 41) and the view of Bath to your left. A diversion to Prior Park Landscape Garden (National Trust) can be taken at the end of the Balcony by going through the kissing gate opposite the steps and down a steep slope for approximately 330 yards (300m) (opening times and admission fee apply). Go past the pond on your left and bear right up steep steps. Continue straight ahead until you re-join the cycle track. Bear left and follow the cycle track, and go through a gap in a stone wall and continue 165 yards (150m) along the cycle track with a field on the right, until you reach a metal kissing gate on the left.

For next directions, turn to page 47

Was 'Capability' Brown once here?

When Ralph Allen's affairs were being settled following his death in 1764, an intriguing receipt for £60 to the famous, naturalistic garden designer Lancelot 'Capability' Brown was discovered (see image, below).

We know Brown was working in the area at the time – but there is no surviving plan, or even a record of a visit to Prior Park. His influence on the Landscape Garden, and possibly also the wider estate, therefore remains a mystery.

Around Prior Park

The carriage drives

Ralph Allen laid out many driveways or rides across his estate, most of which followed the edge of the downs to take advantage of the views. Richard Jones estimated that these drives totalled more than ten miles; they extended as far as Rush Hill and radiated away to the south of Prior Park.

Today only a few fragments survive. Part of a carriage drive to Allen's mansion still runs along below Rainbow Wood. The Dry Arch or Rustic Arch, south-west of Prior Park mansion, used to carry a driveway or coach road west from the house. Others remain in the alignment of some roads in Combe Down and Widcombe.

'The ride bordering the grounds is miles in extent in which the views of the city, river and adjacent country are every minute so varied that to me it wears the appearance of a fairy ground, nothing can be more enchanting.'

Samuel Derrick, Bath's Master of Ceremonies (the successor to Beau Nash), 1763

Left Prior Park in 1750 – this illustration is said to be the earliest depiction of a railway in the UK. Engraving by Anthony Walker, by kind permission of Bath Central Library

PRIOR PARK the Seat of Ralph Allen Esq.r near Bath.   PRIOR PARC la Residence de Raoul Allen Ecuyer pres de Bath

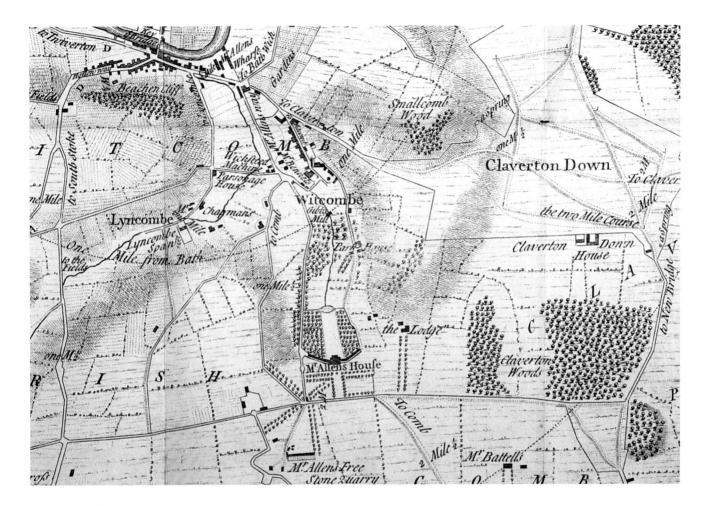

The tree planting

The land here was surveyed in 1742, about the same time Allen moved into Prior Park. The map drawn up shows trees planted in formal arrangements, and avenues of native trees radiating out from a terrace on the mansion's south side.

Allen also established large plantations of Scots pine and spruce trees on Bathampton Down, at the top of Widcombe Hill and across Combe Down. According to Richard Jones, 55,146 fir trees were planted and, since they were on the bare skyline, they made a considerable impact, described as 'the pride and ornament of the surrounding county' (Somerset historian Reverend John Collinson (1757–93)). Combe Down, the site of Allen's mines, was developed into a site for convalescent homes because of the reputed ability of the fir trees to add a particularly healthy quality to the air in the neighbourhood. Later, as the trees matured, they were used to provide pit props and deal boards for house construction. But after 1809, the plantations were cut down on a large scale; few of the trees survive today.

Above A section of a 1742 map by Thomas Thorpe, showing Claverton Down. The full map shows Bath and the five miles surrounding it on each side. It was drawn up to help the discerning carriage traveller follow the fashion for exploring the countryside

Smallcombe Vale and Wood

Smallcombe Vale

The Roman sacred pilgrimage settlement of Aquae Sulis had many wealthy visitors and the Skyline's productive farmland would have sustained inhabitants. There would have been local farms, stone houses for stewards and overseers and villas with estates, perhaps set in a designed landscape among the ancient field systems. The villas themselves would have occupied the heads of sheltered valleys and had grand views.

A scatter of Roman finds were discovered in Smallcombe Vale, perhaps giving a clue to the location of one such villa. Another is likely to have been situated on Rainbow Wood Farm on Claverton Down (see page 36).

Smallcombe Wood

Smallcombe Wood is a little off the main Bath Skyline trail, but well worth the diversion. This is one of Bath's few ancient woodlands, which means it has been here for at least 400 years. The veteran oak, small-leaved lime and ash trees crowd together with dogwoods and guelder rose, but through them you can still catch glimpses of the city.

Although popular with locals and dog walkers, the area feels forgotten. Moss creeps over stone walls and greenery encroaches on paths. Once part of a picturesque shrubbery laid out for Number 6 Woodland Place , a 19th-century, now-empty eight-foot (2.5-metre) square slate pool hints of a grander past. It may have been used to supply water to a circular fountain, also part of the now-abandoned garden.

Watch out for birds such as nuthatches, wrens and blackcaps. In early summer, you might spot some rarer plants, including gladdon, Solomon's seal and bee orchids.

🔟 Go through the kissing gate and take extra care while going down the steep slope through the woodland as after 330 yards (300m) the path opens on to to a busy main road (Widcombe Hill) at the bottom. Carefully cross over the road on to the pavement, turn left and continue down the road with a field and views to the right and Georgian houses on the left. Turn right into the field (Smallcombe Vale) through a metal kissing gate opposite Prospect road.

For a short diversion here to Smallcombe Wood, bear slightly right and continue along the grass path to reach the woodland ahead of you. From here, you can also visit Smallcombe Garden Cemetery (see page 48). Retrace your footsteps to rejoin the main Skyline walk.

Almost immediately on your left, go through another metal kissing gate. Walk diagonally downhill across the field keeping the views in front of you. Bear right until reaching a metal kissing gate next to a water trough. Go through the kissing gate into a field and follow the path down the steps with the Nuttery fence to the left.

Opposite A view over Smallcombe Vale

Left In Smallcombe Wood, keep your eye out for nuthatches

Smallcombe Garden Cemetery
The Nuttery
Richens Orchard

Smallcombe Garden Cemetery

Until recently Smallcombe Garden Cemetery was almost a ruin. Walls were falling down and headstones removed in case they fell on visitors. Bath was in real danger of losing part of its heritage.

Then, in 2014, with the aid of a Heritage Lottery Fund grant, a restoration project was begun. Walls were repaired and made safe, and grass-management plans implemented. In autumn 2015, the site was joined up to Smallcombe Wood via new steps and a stile, making it an easy-to-reach digression from the Skyline walk.

Nature through the seasons

The cemetery's yew, hazel and cherry laurel trees attract jays and other woodland birds, while buzzards circle overhead. The quaking and tor grasses next to the paths provide food for ringlet butterflies and other invertebrates.

One hundred species of lichen grow on the headstones and memorials. Spring brings with it wild primroses and, in wooded areas, the unmistakable scent of wild garlic. You might also spot the pale lilac coralroot; in the West Country it is restricted to woodland gardens, but the colony at Smallcombe is an exception.

Who's buried here?

Arguably the cemetery's most renowned resident is Frederic E. Weatherley (1848–1929), who wrote the lyrics of well-known songs including 'Danny Boy' and 'Roses of Picardy'. However there are many other fascinating stories hidden among the graves. This includes Major Charles Edward Davis (1827–1902), former city architect and surveyor, who designed the prominent, and contentious, six-storey Empire Hotel on the Grand Parade in Bath (art historian Sir Nikolaus Pevsner described it as a 'monstrosity and unbelievable piece of pompous architecture'). Davis also discovered elements of the original Roman baths.

Left A bird of prey glides in the skies over the Skyline

Below Smallcombe Garden Cemetery

Also buried here are two recipients of the Victoria Cross: Lieutenant George Fosbery was awarded it in 1863 for his 'valiant leadership' during the Umbeyla Expedition in India, and Commander Henry Raby of the Royal Navy was decorated in 1855 in honour of his heroism during the Crimean War.

The Nuttery

As you walk down the slope of the lower field of Smallcombe Vale, take a look at the Nuttery. This was established in 2009 when 37 trees were planted: 25 cob nuts, 6 walnuts, 3 sweet chestnuts, 3 almonds and 3 bush varieties: medlar, quince and a mulberry.

Richens Orchard

On leaving the first of the Bathwick Fields, you enter Richens Orchard. Set up in 2005, it contains 45 apple, plum and pear trees featuring local varieties with fantastic names such as Ashmead's Kernel, Tom Putt, Beauty of Bath, Worcester Pearmain and Reverend W. Wilkes.

Walking directions *(map on front flap)*

11 Go through a metal kissing gate at the bottom of the hill and cross the lane. Go through a wooden gate opposite and continue up the steep path and steps. Bear right then follow the path as it bends sharply to the left. Go through the metal kissing gate into the field. Continue up the slope until Bath comes back into view. Bear right keeping the views on your left. Keep to the left as the path forks and continue to the metal kissing gate into Richens Orchard. Cross the top of the orchard to another metal kissing gate opposite. Continue through the next field keeping the wooden fence to the left and head for the metal kissing gate. Go through the kissing gate. The grassy path forks straight after the gate: keep to the right path and continue 220 yards (200m) across the field until reaching a metal kissing gate next to a larger wooden gate and a wide path beyond. Exit the field and continue straight ahead for 44 yards (40m) until you reach the National Trust bus stop, where you will be back at the start of the walk.

Above Apples growing in Richens Orchard

Family Discovery Trail

See pages 52–3 for more information

—— Family Discovery Trail

- - - Connecting footpaths

 Access to the trail

A **Woodland Play Area** Climbing tree, rope walk, scramble net, climbing rope, log pole challenge, rope swing, log seesaw, build a den and make some wild art

B **Long Wood Elf and Fairy Foray** Discover the doors to 15 elf and fairy homes along 0.25 miles (400m) of woodland

C **The Balcony Challenge** Find the biggest hammock made by our yellow meadow ants and collect leaves of all shapes and colours!

D **Klondyke Field Forage** Hunt for bugs, pick blackberries (Aug–Oct) and make a grass trumpet

E **The Hadley Arms Public House** Children welcome! Tel: 01225 837117

F **Darling Deli** Café offering handmade and organic fare
Tel: 01225 835118
www.darlingdeli.co.uk
Co-operative Food Store

G **Prior Park Visitor Reception** Drinks and toilets available during opening hours. Tel: 01225 833422

 Picnic area

 Bus stop

WC Toilets

 Visitor Centre

 Cycle route

 Refreshments

 Viewpoint

National Trust threshold signs

Please note
- The trail is not staffed
- We advise that all activities are supervised by an adult

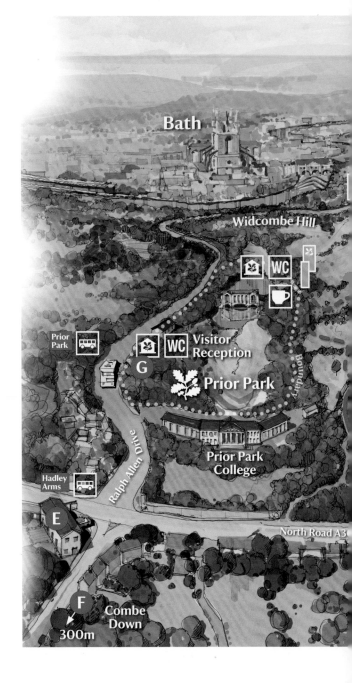

Sham Castle

University
of Bath

Bathwick Hill

Copseland

Widcombe
Hill/Oakley

Rainbow
Wood Farm

Claverton Down Road

Klondyke
Field

D

Rainbow
Wood Farm

N

Claverton Down

Steps

C

The
alcony

Woodland
Play Area

A

Long Wood Elf and
Fairy Foray

Larch Wood

B

Bath
Clinic

Shaft
Road

Claverton Down Road

Ralph Allen
School

Flatwoods
Road

50m

Exploring the Family Discovery Trail

This accessible, two-mile walk is ideal for those with buggies and wheelchairs, or for families without the time to take on the longer Skyline walk.

Set on level ground on mostly smooth surfaces, this trail was designed with accessibility in mind – although it should be noted that there are a couple of short sections through unsurfaced fields.

Although shorter than the Skyline walk, visitors won't miss out on much of what makes the longer route so special: nature, stunning views back across Bath and an escape from the lively city.

Woodland trails

There are activity stations to find as you make your way along the walk.

Long Wood Elf and Fairy Foray

Along the trail are the doors to the houses of 15 elf and fairy folk. You might stumble across the home of mischievous Bold Saturnleaf or Pumpkin Watersprite, who has sat on his flying pumpkin for a thousand years. But please don't try to open their doors – their magic keeps them shut tight while they're out and about.

Alphabet trail

Fourteen letters are hidden at intervals along the two-mile (three-kilometre) walk. Try to find them all, and work out which of the fairy or elf names they spell.

How to get here

- Catch the City Sightseeing Skyline Tour Bus from Bath Spa Railway station. From here, you have two options.
- Alight Stop M (Claverton Down Road): Cross the road and turn left for about 22 yards (20m). You will find National Trust signs by a gate on your right. Go through the gate, follow the signs to the Woodland Play Area. Go through the play area to enjoy the Elf and Fairy Foray.
- Alight at Stop N (Ralph Allen School). Cross the road and go through the gate into Long Wood Field. Walk straight ahead along the edge of the field, then pass through another gate on to a woodland path. Turn right on to the Elf and Fairy Foray. Pass through the Foray to find the Woodland Play Area.
- Please note, both stops are request stops – so make sure you ring the bell to let the driver know that you want to get off.

Woodland Play Area

Pop up your feet with a thermos as the kids enjoy the high swing, log seesaw, scramble net and much more in this purpose-built Woodland Play Area.

Tick off your '50 Things'

The family trail is the perfect spot to make some wild art or a trail with sticks or build a den. In autumn and winter, why not try to catch a falling leaf, fly a kite or splash in a puddle. You will find fields perfect for foraging: you can hunt for bugs all year round, and from September to November you'll find gluts of blackberries just ripe for picking. You can also take part in geocaching.

Above and opposite, bottom Some of the fairies whose houses you might encounter in the Woodland Play Area

Opposite Catching butterflies

Above Children playing in the Woodland Play Area

Nature Across the Skyline

One of the walk's great attractions and joys is the variety of nature you'll see, even in the depths of winter: from mammals to birds and butterflies, from wild flowers to trees.

Skyline botany

Depending on the time of year, you'll find woodlands full of spring flowers; grassland slopes on lime-rich soils covered in summer with attractive carpets of downland plants; wide tracts of flower-rich hay meadow, and all the mysteries of ancient woodlands with their rich mixture of mosses, liverworts, ferns and fungi.

Ancient woodland

You can tell when you are in ancient woodland by its structure. Tall oaks and ash trees form the canopy, with an understorey of hazel that has been coppiced over many centuries to provide timber. Smallcombe Wood is one of the best examples along the Skyline walk.

The ground flora is dominated in spring by swathes of wild garlic, with patches of bluebells and wood anemone. The wild service tree, spindle, spurge laurel, dog's mercury and yellow archangel are all indicative of ancient woodland, and there are several unusual species, including coralroot and parasitic toothwort.

Grasslands

Limestone grasslands provide some of the botanical highlights of the walk. Here in the close-knit turf grow a great number of species, mostly flowering plants rather than grasses.

Several fields on the hillside above Prior Park and Sham Castle Down below Sham Castle are outstanding examples. In spring they are covered in primroses and cowslips, but perhaps the best time to see them is in June and July when the orchids are in flower. The most frequently seen species are the common spotted orchid, with dark spots on its leaves, and the bright pink pyramidal orchid. Both form striking patches in these slopes. Another is the bee orchid, mimicking a bee precisely; it tends to occur singly and is more scattered.

The limestone grassland areas are dominated by yellow, due to an abundance of bird's foot trefoil, black medick and a variety of yellow composites, particularly rough hawkbit, smooth hawksbeard and the paler yellow and smaller mouse-ear hawkweed. Other yellow flowers include upright spikes of agrimony and sprawling heads of yellow bedstraw.

Salad burnet occurs everywhere, together with a scattering of the tiny white fairy flax and occasionally smart little flowers of eyebright. Red clover is abundant and patches of thyme may occasionally be found on the tops of anthills.

Other flowers include yarrow, small scabious, the tiny cut-leaved cranesbill, and patches of a small umbellifer called pignut. There are thistles too. Dwarf thistles are inconspicuous until

Opposite, clockwise from top left The bee orchid's similarity in appearance to bees is no accident; the flowers evolved to attract bees as an aid to pollination, but in the UK the flowers are self-pollinating

Common knapweed flowers are attractive to butterflies

Fine-leaved grasses in the limestone grasslands

Cowslip is an early spring flower

Ribwort plantain in flower

Pyramidal orchids provide a splash of colour

you sit on one, but you can't miss the striking architecture of the rare, tall, limestone-loving woolly thistle.

Grasses are predominantly fine-leaved species such as fescues, upright brome, yellow oat grass and the striking, delicate quaking grass. Both ribwort and hoary plantain are abundant, a striking feature when in full flower.

Meadows
A field cut for its hay is called a meadow and a field grazed exclusively by farm animals is termed pasture. Our hay meadows at Bathwick Fields and Smallcombe Vale are covered in cowslips in spring and buttercups in early summer, but they become much more diverse by August. Unimproved patches may include some unusual species, such as corky-fruited water dropwort.

Walls and paths
Maidenhair spleenwort and hart's tongue fern can often be seen growing on stone walls and there is always a mixture of wild flowers growing along the paths, including dog rose, cow parsley, burdock, teasel and evening primrose.

Skyline animals

Walking the Skyline, you will be struck by the great variety of landscapes encountered. There are open expanses of hay meadow with parkland trees, and narrow paths fringed with cow parsley, long-established limestone grasslands and ancient woodlands where the path winds in places between crags, hollows and caves of old quarries. These provide a rich variety of habitats for birds, butterflies and other insects, and mammals, even including some rare bats.

Birds

With wide vistas and open skies you will often hear the mewing calls of buzzards and deep croaks of ravens. In summer, swifts and house martins feed low over the meadows and the songs of small warblers, blackcaps and chiffchaffs ring out along tree-lined paths. Jays show their white flashes as they dash for cover, and you may spot the rounded wings and long tail of a sparrow hawk circling above.

Woodpigeons are everywhere, but their lesser-known relative the stock dove can also be heard in a few places – a rather strained cooing high up in old beech trees where it nests in holes.

Clockwise from far left
Chiffchaffs pick insects from trees and also fly out to snap them up when the insect is in flight

A male orange-tip butterfly (females do not have orange on their wings)

The greater horseshoe bat is the largest horseshoe bat in Europe

A grasshopper at Prior Park

The common buzzard's mewing call might be mistaken for a cat's

Another unusual woodland bird is the marsh tit, recognised by its shiny black cap and buff plumage. Listen also for woodpeckers. A sharp staccato 'chip' announces the great spotted woodpecker, a smart bird with black and white plumage and bright red under the tail. The ringing laugh of a green woodpecker carries much further. It is most often seen searching for ants on areas of short turf, but when disturbed all you see is its yellow rump as it flies off.

Bushes along the wayside support whitethroats, with their excited scratchy song flight, and you may well hear the soft 'peeoo' of a bullfinch and catch a glimpse of its bright red breast. Crows and magpies along with flocks of jackdaws occur throughout the year. And occasionally a red kite may appear.

Butterflies

Springtime sees the appearance of the first butterflies, notably the bright yellow brimstone and the smaller orange-tip.

Some of the best places to find butterflies in summer are the herb-rich meadows on steep slopes where you can spot a meadow brown, ringlet, common blue, gatekeeper, comma, and marbled white. Sometimes day-flying burnet moths are seen feeding on knapweed. Speckled wood butterflies vie for territory along woodland paths and the holly blue may well be seen along ivy-covered walls.

Insects

Rough grassland and odd corners with bramble, burdock, hogweed and teasel attract a variety of insects, especially dark bush crickets with their rasping song. Others include many kinds of hoverflies, bees and parasitic wasps. In places, the grasslands are covered in large anthills created by yellow meadow ants, giving these steep slopes a very special character. A nationally rare species, the downland bee-fly, was also recently discovered here.

Mammals

Along the walk you may see roe deer, foxes and badgers, but much depends on the time of day. Early morning and late evening are best for seeing deer, but a fox may be seen lying up in broad daylight, off the beaten track and away from dogs. There are badger setts in places along much of the walk. The larger setts are very obvious, but it requires much patience at nightfall to see the badgers. (Note: badgers are a protected species, and their setts shouldn't be disturbed.)

Bats

Bats need specialist equipment for identification, but the area is notable for a number of species, including the lesser horseshoe and brown long-eared. A cave close to the Skyline walk in Bathampton Wood provides an important roosting site for nationally scarce greater horseshoe bats. Management of meadows by cattle grazing encourages dung beetles, an important food source for the larger bats.

Clockwise from top left
Soldier beetles feeding on a flower head

The green woodpecker is the largest of the three woodpeckers that breed in the UK

The common blue damselfly is usually seen from April to September, and possibly into October

Wildlife spotter's guide

Early purple orchid

Marsh tit

Yellow meadow ant

Gatekeeper butterfly

Dung beetle

Beech

Common blue butterfly

Lady's bedstraw

Lapwing

Speckled wood butterfly

Starling

Comma butterfly

Self heal

Meadow brown butterfly

Greater spotted woodpecker

Redwing

Greater horseshoe bat

Ringlet butterfly

Dark bush cricket

Day flying burnet moth

Common spotted orchid

Red kite

Ash

Yellow brimstone butterfly

Fieldfare

Oak

Marbled white butterfly

Meadow pipit

Looking After the Skyline

So important is the Skyline to the character and heritage of Bath, it has been included within the boundary of the World Heritage Site.

The Trust's approach to managing this rich pastoral countryside is to balance the needs of access with the vital role of conservation, so as to safeguard what is so valuable about this landscape – its unique character, important archaeological history and valuable properties for plants and animals. We are committed to preserving this special landscape for wildlife and for future generations to appreciate.

We employ traditional countryside management techniques where possible, such as laying our hedges to extend their lives and make them as attractive as possible to the many species that depend on them. Many miles of stone walls are cared for with the help of highly experienced volunteer teams and specialist contractors. They not only preserve these important landscape features, but also help to keep alive the rural traditions that make for a living landscape.

Preserving a wildlife-rich landscape

Since the Second World War, over 95% of the country's natural meadows have been lost. This highlights how important sensitive management of wildlife-rich landscapes like the Skyline is today.

Wildflower-rich grasslands are promoted through sensitive grazing – the right number of sheep and cattle at the right time of year. If this grazing is managed just right over many years it will keep down the fast growing grasses, giving space for the rarer, more fragile flowers to thrive.

Over winter, volunteers help us to preserve these important limestone grasslands by controlling the spread of scrub through a sensitive programme of cutting and clearance.

The hay meadows follow the traditional annual cycle that has remain unchanged for centuries: grass and flowers grow undisturbed until mid-July, by which time they will have set seed. The fields are then cut and hay bales are made for feeding cattle at the farm later in the season. Following a short fallow period, to allow some further growth, grazing is introduced in the last part of the season – usually September to November. On the steeper fields the farm animals are removed over the wetter winters to avoid the risk of the ground being churned up.

Our woodlands contain some remarkable specimens, notably of beech but also oak and ash and even elm. These are managed to ensure the woodland flora thrives, by allowing in some light and by selective thinning to benefit trees of particular note.

Above **A National Trust volunteer conservation group working on Little Solsbury Hill**